SIMPLY SCANDINAVIAN

TERO KALLIO   KIMMO SAIRA

SIMPLY SCANDINAVIAN

TRAVELLING IN TIME WITH FINNISH CUISINE AND NATURE

RAIKAS PUBLISHING LTD

CONTENTS

DEAR READER

This book takes you on a journey of two dimensions: tastes and time. You have a chance to acquaint yourself with the Scandinavian countries and primarily with Finnish culinary tastes. At the same time you can enjoy samples of Finland's colourful nature photography. The time theme of the book also has two dimensions. They represent traditional Finnish food and ingredients as well as recipes to the taste of the 21st century. Another dimension in connection with the voyage in time can be found in the structure of the book. The journey into the culinary world of tastes starts with spring and ends with winter. Thus the servings and the recipes in the book are presented according to the seasons which can be seen for example in the choice of ingredients and the illustrations.

The book "Simply Scandinavian – Travelling in Time with Finnish Cuisine and Nature" is not a book of traditional food in the usual sense of the word. Save a few exceptions we have tried to tweak each recipe in some way. An example of this is the liver bake where the flavour of the old-fashioned recipe has been enhanced by adding sherry. In a few recipes we have open-mindedly tried to combine the past and the present. Such a recipe is for example rye cannelloni served in consommé; it contains a pinch of hard times in Finland, a dash of modern universal cooking and a smidgeon of national romanticism. The shape and name of the portion come from Italy, the filling from a Finnish meat pie and the dough from the Karelian pastry from eastern Finland, seasoned with war-time bark flour.

Even in the book's most modern recipes we have tried to be faithful to the Scandinavian tradition. Although the way the food is served might be borrowed from as far away as from Japan, all the ingredients can be grown, gathered, fished, or hunted in the Scandinavian forests and lakes, save a few exceptions. The recipes are also given

an original flare by the rich use of edible plants such as dandelion, birch sap and wood-sorrel.

This book is a picture book. Its center naturally lies in photographs of food, but the structure tied to seasons is also in harmony with the stunning pictures of the Scandinavian nature from the archipelago in southern Finland to the harsh wilderness of Lapland. The recipes in this book are estimated for four persons.

FINLAND IN BRIEF

Finland is situated in northern Europe between the 60th and 70th latitude. The area of the country is 338,000 square kilometres, and is slightly smaller than for example France. Finland's neighbours are Sweden to the west, Norway to the north, and Russia to the east. Finland has a border of more than 1,000 kilometres with Russia, In the south, only a short sea voyage away, is Finland's brother nation Estonia.

In 1917 Finland declared itself independent having been an autonomous part of the Russian empire for about 100 years. The autonomy was very comprehensive: Finland had its own currency, army, mail service and internal government. Until 1809 Finland was part of the Kingdom of Sweden.

The connections to the West and Sweden remained strong even after Finland became an autonomous part of the Russian empire. This was, among other things, due to the fact that a major part of the upper class and merchants were Swedish-speaking. The strong tie to Sweden can still be seen, even if only approximately five per cent of the population speaks Swedish as their mother tongue.

The Finnish culinary culture is unique in many ways. The proximity to both Sweden and Russia have had a strong influence on Finnish food. This is obvious also in the recipes of this book. Examples of this are Beef à la Rydberg and the blini.

At the end of 2007 Finland had a population of 5.3 million. More than one million Finns live in the capital, Helsinki, or in its vicinity in southern Finland. In the northernmost province, Lapland, about 180,000 inhabitants live among them the most famous man in the world: Santa Claus! Lapland also has a population of more than 200,000 reindeer, thus Rudolphs outnumber people!

THE LAND OF A THOUSAND LAKES – AND SAUNAS

Finland is called "The Land of a Thousand Lakes". No wonder; the total number of lakes is approximately 190,000. During summer evenings one can see tiny blue smoke pillars rising here and there from the lake shores – the Finns are heating their national pride, the sauna. It is said that the Finns are born and die in the sauna. Some truth lies in this because as late as in the 1940's many Finns were born in a sauna. The final voyage of many Finns also started in the sauna where the deceased person was washed in preparation for his or her final journey. Only after the influence of the Scandinavian affluent society reached Finland in the 1960's, did the importance of the sauna as the place for entering and leaving the world come to an end. But the sauna is important to the Finns even in the 21st century. Almost every Finnish home – also in blocks of flats – has a sauna, and the hot room which is heated by wood burning or electric stoves is also the heart of Finnish summer cottages. People bathe daily in the sauna especially in the summer. The sauna is also eminently suitable as a place for cooking. One can smoke and dry meat or fish there. Sausage fried on a sauna stove is delicious!

THE WORLD'S LARGEST ARCHIPELAGO

The mosaic of islands in the south-west of Finland stretches out towards the coast of Sweden. The archipelago is one of the largest in the world, at least judging by the number of islands. The harsh landscape of the archipelago westwards from Turku, Finland's fifth largest town, comprises of more than 20,000 islands. Many of these islands are inhibited

all year round. The main sources of livelihood for the inhabitants of the archipelago are farming and fishing.

Before the midsummer celebrations the whole of Finland waits for the first new potatoes which are grown by farmers in the archipelago. These delicacies are sold in market places and supermarkets. The islands' new potatoes ripen earlier than those on the mainland because the warmer climate allows earlier planting of potatoes than in other parts of the country. The festivity of the "nightless night" at midsummer is celebrated in the peace of summer cottages, bathing in the sauna and enjoying new potatoes with pickled herring and other fish (see page 45).

BERRIES, MUSHROOMS, GAME AND FISH

Enormous green forest areas are spreading out below you, and with them blue glittering lakes alternate. Here and there you can see a moose or a bear crossing a marsh. Somewhere smoke from a small village is rising up in the air, or lights from a little town are competing with the darkening summer evening. Such a view can open up beneath you if you decide to travel by air from for example Helsinki to Rovaniemi, the town at the polar circle.

The large forest areas of Finland hide a very versatile food store. In the spring one can for example pick lots of different useful plants to make a salad. The delicacy par excellence of the spring forest is the most sought after mushroom: the false

morel. During the summer delicate berries like blueberry, red bilberry, and cranberry ripen in the forests and on the marshes in the north, and the most exotic of them all grows on the wetlands of Lapland, the cloudberry (see page 90).

Nowadays Finland is one of the world's most prosperous countries. The development has been breathtaking considering that 150 years ago the main livelihood of the Finns besides agriculture, was hunting and fishing. The industrial revolution didn't reach Finland until the early 20th century. Amidst the present prosperity and modern times an outside observer can, however, observe in the behaviour of the Finns signs of times past – a time when hunting, fishing and berry picking were often

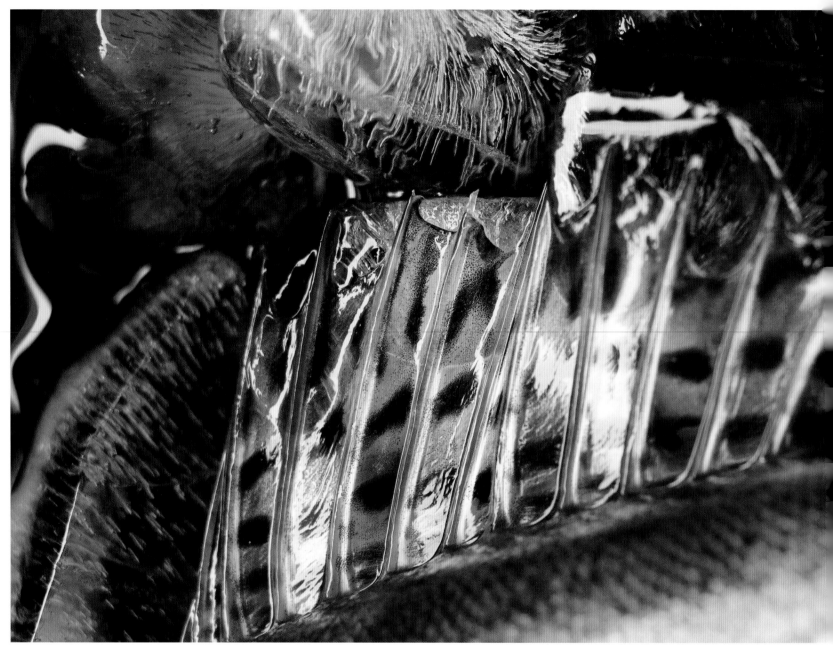

important sources of nourishment beside the often very sparse crop of agriculture. One such sign is the hobby of hunting. And there is a lot to be hunted in the nature of the north. To hunt moose a special licence is required in Finland, and approx. 80,000 such permits are granted annually to prospective hunters.

Popular hunting targets are also fowl, for example capercaillie and black grouse. The population of the first mentioned is, however, sparse in parts of the country. Hunting capercaillie is allowed only for a short time every season and only where the population can sustain hunting.

The pinnacle of the summer for many Finns is the mallard hunt starting at the end of August. At that time one can hear shots fired and dogs barking on the shores of the lakes, when our canine friends run impatiently into the bulrushes to look for the birds their masters have shot.

In the autumn the mushrooms are abundant. After the rains of late summer for example chanterelles, boletus and horns of plenty rear their heads. Each year millions of tons of edible mushrooms that people long for are rotting in the vast forests of Finland. Only about 10 per cent are harvested annually. But that is enough for thousands of gravies, pies and other meals for the winter. Lots of Finnish mushrooms are also exported.

WINTER TIME

During winter Finnish nature rests. At the beginning of December the sun ceases to show its face in Lapland. The period of darkness, the opposite of the nightless night of summer, makes the north dark for two months. The darkness, the northern lights and the white snow create a Christmassy feeling which an ever increasing number of tourists from all over the world enjoy every year.

The serenity of the winter nature is only window dressing. Below the icy cover, there is a buzz of activity in the thousand lakes with for example the burbot rises to spawn in February. At the same time a certain activity can be observed on the ice.

The fishermen have dug out their fishing drills and winter overalls and go out onto the ice to attend to their nets, and also to do some fishing with their jigs. The catch comprises of perch, pike-perch, burbot, pike, and whitefish.

SCANDINAVIAN DESIGN AND FOOD, CLOSE TO NATURE

Finland and other Scandinavian nations have a special relationship with nature. Nature is where we come from, and nature is where we always want to return. Especially during the summer holiday season and weekends towns are deserted when people travel to the countryside to enjoy its peaceful atmosphere.

Closeness to nature can also be seen in Finnish and Scandinavian design. It is uncomplicated and practical. The same goes for the food, thus the name "Simply Scandinavian". The Finns do not spend too much energy on complicated cooking processes. The secret of delicacy is often in only a few basic ingredients of the highest quality, and in a long cooking time.

The Finns are genuine and honest – just like the creations of the giants of Finnish design, Alvar Aalto and Timo Sarpaneva, shown here in photographs. Also, modesty and the pursuit of modesty, are an inseparable part of the Finnish national character. Due to their modesty the Finns seldom feel comfortable in the limelight, nor do they speak very loud in a discussion group. Being modest can also be a drawback, as you will never be noticed unless you promote your talent a little.

Dear reader, now it's time to send you off on a fascinating journey of flavours of the traditional and modern Finnish cuisine with its many delicacies. As authors of this book, and on behalf of all Finns, we hope that the recipes, texts, and pictures will bring joy and new culinary stimuli to all readers.

Tero Kallio and Kimmo Saira

SPRING

In spring nature, animals and people waken to life. The forest turns green. People work on their fields and on their allotments. Even animals awake to courtship. The Scandinavian spring vegetation has much to offer in terms of delicacies: dandelion, sorrel, annual shoots of spruce, and birch sap are superb ingredients for cooking. The three first-mentioned give flavour to e.g. salads and from the latter you can make syrup or drink it almost as such. But one stands out superbly: the king of forest mushrooms, the morel.

SPRING APPETIZERS

The false morel is one of the most delicious mush-rooms in the world. It grows generally on logging areas of the forest or in their vicinity. Do not go into the woods in the autumn to look for false morels as, unlike other Finnish mushrooms, the false morel grows only in the spring.

This recipe follows that of a classical mushroom soup. But it has a surprising element: the coffee gives the soup a unique flavour highlighting the superb taste of the false morel.

FALSE MOREL SOUP WITH COFFEE

1 LITRE (4 CUPS) FRESH FALSE MORELS
1 ONION
1 TABLESPOON BUTTER
PLAIN WHEAT FLOUR
400 ML (13.5 FL OZ) CREAM
100 ML (3.4 FL OZ) COFFEE
½ TEASPOON SUGAR
500 ML (17 FL OZ) WATER
1 VEGETABLE STOCK CUBE
BLACK PEPPER CORNS

Parboil the morels twice, 10 minutes each time. Rinse between the parboils. Do not use the parboiling water for cooking, it is poisonous! After the second parboil, rinse the morels in cold water and shake until dry.

Prepare the vegetable stock by melting the stock cube in boiling water. Chop the morels and the onion. Pour the morels into a medium hot frying pan and fry lightly until their natural moisture has evaporated. Add the butter and the onion. Fry the morels and the onion for a couple of minutes.

When the onion has softened slightly, sprinkle the flour over the contents of the frying pan and mix with a spatula into an even paste. Add the stock, stirring constantly. Simmer for 10 minutes. Add the cream, coffee, sugar, a pinch of salt and freshly ground black pepper. Bring to the boil. Taste for flavour and serve.

*Spring is the season for celebrations and what is a celebration without champagne! A perfect companion to this soup is the slightly richer **Blondel Brut Carte d'Or.***

17

The Scandinavian nature is abundant of all kinds of edible plants. Many of them are used in a salad almost au naturel. In the spring the dandelion covers the roadsides and lawns. No wonder that it is considered a weed! But the dandelion makes a delicious, unique and beautiful spring salad. The sorrel gives the salad a primitive special flavour.

DANDELION SALAD

FEAT. WALDORF

Pick young dandelion leaves. Wash them carefully and cut the leaves lengthwise. Discard the main leaf vein. Use only the soft parts of the leaves. Wash then oakleaf lettuce, celery, grapes and sorrel. Halve the grapes, cut the celery into 5 mm (0.2 inch) thick slices. Peel the apple and cut into small cubes. Roughly shread the lettuce. Chop the walnuts in a food processor. Leave a few whole nuts for decoration. Mix all the ingredients in a bowl, decorate with dandelion flowers and whole walnuts.

Mix the yoghurt, creamy sour milk, cream, honey and olive oil. Season with ground black pepper.

SALAD:
2 LITRES (8 CUPS) FRESH DANDELION LEAVES
1 POT OAKLEAF LETTUCE
½ POT WHEAT SPROUTS
2 CELERY STALKS
150 ML (⅗ CUP) WALNUTS
200 ML (⅘ CUP) BLUE GRAPES
1 APPLE
50 ML (3 TABLESPOONS) SORREL

DRESSING:
200 ML (7 FL OZ) NATURAL YOGHURT
200 ML (7 FL OZ) CREAMY SOUR MILK
1 TEASPOON LIQUID HONEY
1 TABLESPOON OLIVE OIL
GROUND BLACK PEPPER

*The Austrian gift to the wine-drinkers of the world are white wines made from the grape Grüner Veltliner. The freshness and fruitiness of the Grüner go well with a salad. This time we chose a **Bründlmeyer Ried Loiser Berg Grüner Veltliner.***

A sandwich cake loaf is very commonly used in Scandinavia. However, other than at graduation, birthday and other big parties it is almost never served. This is probably due to the fact that a cake loaf is cumbersome to make and to prepare it for a smaller group is not considered worthwhile. This recipe gives you an alternative: a petite sandwich cake is quick to make and a superb appetizer considering its size.

PETIT SANDWICH CAKE

Chop the crayfish tails and dill. Add the crème fraiche and the creamy sour milk. Mix and taste. Chop the chives finely and flake the hotsmoked salmon with a fork. Add the mayonnaise and the lemon juice to the salmon and chives. Mix and taste.

    Cut the slices of bread into circles using a timbale. Place a slice of whole grain brown bread at the bottom of the timbale. Add a layer of approximately 1 cm (0.4 inch) of the salmon-mayonnaise mix. In order that the light fish and crayfish pastes will distinguish colourwise from the bread, the middle slice of bread should also be a rye one. Spread crayfish paste on the middle slice of bread. Add a slice of white bread. Press the cake out of the timbale. Cover the top-most slice of bread with a thin layer of mayonnaise. Decorate with coldsmoked salmon and dill.

8 SLICES DARK WHOLE GRAIN BREAD
4 SLICES WHITE BREAD FOR TOASTING
200 G (7 OZ) EUROPEAN CRAYFISH TAILS
250 G (9 OZ) HOTSMOKED SALMON OR ARCTIC CHAR
100 G (3.5 OZ) COLDSMOKED SALMON
1 TABLESPOON CREAMY SOUR MILK
2 TABLESPOONS CRÈME FRAICHE
200 ML (7 FL OZ) MAYONNAISE
DILL
CHIVES
1 TABLESPOON LEMON JUICE

Smokiness of the salmon combined with a distinctive rye flavor from the bread can be difficult to match a wine to. **Hartwall 1836 Gourmet beer** *is a result of collaboration between a brewing master and a head chef. Their goal was to make a beer that would compliment different fish dishes. Petit Sandwich Cake and 1836 Gourmet beer is a truly wonderful match.*

SPRING MAIN COURSES

This recipe is one of the more modern and international ones in this book. The roots of pesto are in the Italian cuisine. But here we have no "ordinary" Italian basil pesto. The nettles, the stinging weed and tormentor, does extremely well in a pesto as its slightly bitter taste has a distant resemblance of rucola lettuce. The sweet beetroots, together with the salty pesto, complements the taste of this vegetarian meal.

NETTLE PESTO PASTA

BEETROOT BURGER

Parboil the nettle leaves in boiling water. Rinse and dry. Chop the nettles finely in a food processor together with the garlic and sunflower seeds lightly toasted in a frying pan. Set aside. Grate or chop the cheese in a food processor. Mix the cheese, oil and spices with the nettle paste. Put the pasta in boiling water. Let boil until the pasta is al dente. Drain and mix with the pesto.

Grate the beetroots and mix with the other ingredients. Fry a sample burger in butter. Taste for flavour. Fry the rest of the burgers.

*The sweet taste of cooked beetroots and the "green" taste of the nettles will go well with a red wine from a warm country. **Cave de Tain l'Hermitage Crozes Hermitage** is extremely suitable.*

PESTO:
2–3 LITERS (8–12 CUPS) FRESH LEAVES OF NETTLE
100 ML (⅖ CUP) SUNFLOWER SEEDS
2 GARLIC CLOVES
70 G (2.5 OZ) PARMESAN CHEESE
SUNFLOWER OIL
BLACK PEPPER
A PINCH OF SALT
400 G (14 OZ) PASTA
1 LITRE (2 PT) WATER

BEETROOT BURGERS:
3 MEDIUM SIZED BEETROOTS
1 EGG
50 ML (1.7 FL OZ) CREAM
100 ML (⅖ CUP) DRY BREADCRUMBS
A LITTLE WHITE WINE
SALT
WHITE PEPPER
1 TABLESPOON BUTTER

Dill stew is traditional Finnish food with a good reputation which has undergone some ups and downs. No wonder – the dill stew served in many schools reminds Finnish school-children more of a big lump of meat rather than dill gravy and meat, made with great care. "Real" dill stew is, however, quite different. It is tasty, and with slight perfections it is even a meal for festive occasions.

DILL STEW

MEAT:
800 G (28 OZ/1.8 LB) SHOULDER OR PRIME RIB OF BEEF
WATER
2 TABLESPOONS BUTTER
2 CARROTS
1 ONION
4 DRIED ALLSPICE BERRIES
2 BAY LEAVES
SALT

GRAVY:
300 ML (10 FL OZ) BEEF STOCK
100 ML (3.4 FL OZ) WHITE WINE
1 TEASPOON LEMON JUICE
½ TEASPOON WHITE VINEGAR
1 TEASPOON SUGAR
50 ML (3 TABLESPOONS) PLAIN WHEAT FLOUR
50 ML (1.7 FL OZ) CREAM
1 EGG YOLK
200 ML (4/5 CUP) FINELY CHOPPED DILL
SALT

Boil the water. Put the beef into a pot and cover it completely with boiling water seasoned with salt and butter. Butter seasons but also prevents the meat from going dry. Bring to the boil. Using a perforated ladle, skim off the scum as it rises to the surface. Add the chopped vegetables, allspice berries and bay leaves. Cover the pot and simmer for an hour. Remove the beef from the pot and wrap it in foil together with a bit of butter. Cook it in the oven at 150 °C (300 °F) for 20 minutes. Leave the beef to rest for five minutes after you have removed it from the oven.

Strain the beef stock. Put a saucepan with the stock on the cooker and add the white wine, lemon juice, vinegar, sugar and salt. Stir for a while and add the flour mixed with water for thickening. Bring to the boil. Add the cream and egg yolk, mixed together. Taste for flavour. If the gravy is still too acidy, add a pinch of salt and sugar. Add the chopped dill just before serving. Serve with boiled potatoes.

*The taste of the dill together with the beef makes the choice of white wine difficult. Pinot Noir grapes, however, welcome this challenge. Our choice is **Jackson Estate Pinot Noir from New Zealand.***

*East meets west in this modern recipe.
The meal is very Finnish considering the
ingredients, but the way of frying the fish
is exactly the same as of frying fresh tuna.
The green horseradish cream, on the other
hand, reminds us of Japanese wasabi,
considering its colour as well as its taste.*

GRILLED RAW SPICED SALMON

GREEN PEA SALAD

Rinse the salad ingredients and mix them in a bowl.
Drizzle the balsamic vinegar and the olive oil over
the salad.

Whip the fridge-cool cream thick. Be careful
not to make butter of it! Peel and grate or finely
mince the horseradish in a food processor. Purée
the thawed peas by pressing them through a sieve.
Mix the whipped cream, minced horseradish and
puréed peas. Add a pinch of salt and mix.

Cut the salmon from its skin with a sharp
filleting knife. Cut into steaks. Fry the steaks in
olive oil in a hot frying pan of cast iron for a minute
on each side. Leave the steaks raw in the middle.
Season lightly with salt and white pepper.

SALAD:
500 G (18 OZ/1.1 LB) RAW SPICED SALMON
OLIVE OIL
1 POT PEA SPROUTS
100 G (3.5 OZ) SUGAR SNAP PEAS
1 POT LETTUCE (E.G. RUCOLA, OR OTHER)
100 ML (2/5 CUP) FROZEN OR FRESH GREEN PEAS
BALSAMIC VINEGAR

HORSERADISH CREAM:
100 ML (3.4 FL OZ) DOUBLE CREAM
A SMALL PIECE OF HORSERADISH (SIZE OF A FOREFINGER)
100 ML (⅖ CUP) FROZEN GREEN PEAS

*The slightly oily salmon, strong in taste, and the refreshing
pea salad are a challenging combination for choosing a
wine. A Riesling white wine should go well with the meal
as it suits both elements. We chose a **Léon Beyer Riesling.***

Fried diced meat or sausage with onions and potatoes is a traditional meal made out of left-over ingredients. Many Finns like it, especially when having a hang-over. Beef à la Rydberg, however, is a version of this dish made of only fresh and the best ingredients. It's said that Beef à la Rydberg is originally a Swedish recipe. It may be so, but it tastes good all over Scandinavia.

BEEF À LA RYDBERG

ONIONS IN LAGER, MUSTARD CRÈME

500 G (18 OZ/1.1 LB) INNER FILLET OF BEEF
PICKLED BEETROOTS
PICKLED CUCUMBER
200 ML (6.8 FL OZ) DOUBLE CREAM
1 TEASPOON DIJON MUSTARD
500 G (18 OZ/1.1 LB) FIRM POTATOES (E.G. NICOLA)
2 ONIONS
50 ML (1.7 FL OZ) LAGER
40 G (1.4 OZ) BUTTER
4 EGGS
SALT
BLACK PEPPER CORNS

Cut the beetroots and cucumbers into cubes and leave on a plate. Whip the cream. Add the mustard and mix. Leave to rest in the fridge.

Peel the potatoes. Cut them into cubes the size of your fingertip. Chop the onions. Cut the beef (room-temperature) into cubes slightly bigger than the potatoes. Melt half of the butter in a roaster or a frying pan. Add the potatoes. They will be ready in 10–15 minutes depending on the size of the cubes. Salt will be a sufficient seasoning.

Fry the onions lightly in butter. Add the lager when the onions start to soften and turn down the heat. The onions are ready when the beer has evaporated. Add a pinch of salt.

Melt some butter in a cast iron pot. Add the steak. We chose inner fillet of beef, which will make the dish tastier if the meat is not well done. Frying in a hot pan for a couple of minutes will be enough. Season with salt and black pepper corns.

Separate the egg yolks from the whites. Serve the yolk from the egg shell as a dip for the beef. Serve the dish with pickled beetroots and cucumbers.

Tip: if cooking the meat, potatoes and onions at the same time seems difficult you can cook them one at a time and keep the onions and potatoes warm in the oven at 80 °C (176 °F) while you fry the meat.

*When you use vinegar for cooking, a cold beer is an excellent choice for a drink. We chose **Olvi Sandels**, rich in taste, to complement this meal.*

SPRING DESSERTS

Pancakes can be served with either a salty or a sweet filling. Scandinavians often prefer the latter. In the summer hundreds of thousands of Finns light their barbeques and cook pancakes on a griddle above the flames of the grill. Birch sap syrup is a tasty alternative to, for instance, maple syrup.

PANCAKES

BIRCH SAP SYRUP

PANCAKES:
2 EGGS
500 ML (17 FL OZ) MILK
300 ML (1 ¼ CUPS) PLAIN WHEAT FLOUR
3 TABLESPOONS SUGAR
1 TEASPOON SALT
BUTTER

SYRUP:
1 LITRE (2.1 PT) BIRCH SAP
100 ML (⅖ CUP) BROWN SUGAR

Pour the birch sap into a saucepan. Add the brown sugar. Simmer and reduce the mixture to approximately 250 ml. Leave to cool in the fridge. Serve with the pancakes.

Crack the eggs and whisk them thoroughly. Add half of the milk, sugar and salt. Add the flour, work it in well. Add the rest of the milk. Leave to rest for about 10 minutes. Fry the batter in butter in a frying pan.

Dark roast coffee will go well with the pancakes.

Sweet and sour smoothie is an excellent summer drink. This drink is full of friendly lactic bacteria. Following a heavy barbeque meal, will be a great "digestive" and keep the tummy in order. Vodka adds a kick to the drink and makes it nicely "shottish".

RHUBARB SMOOTHIE

500 G (18 OZ/1.1 LB) RHUBARB
500 ML (17 FL OZ) WATER
200 ML (⅘ CUP) SUGAR
4 TABLESPOONS VODKA
500 ML (17 FL OZ) NATURAL YOGHURT
100 ML (3.4 FL OZ) SOUR MILK
LEAVES OF FRESH LEMON BALM

Peel the rhubarb and cut into pieces 5 cm (2 inch) long. Pour the water into a saucepan, add 50 ml (3 tablespoons) sugar and bring to the boil. Add the rhubarb to the boiling water. Boil until it has softened (approximately 5 minutes) and strain. Add the rest of the sugar and the vodka to the rhubarb, mix and chill in the fridge.

Pour the yoghurt, sour milk and rhubarb paste into a food processor. Mix for a while to add air to the smoothie. Decorate with leaves of lemon balm. Serve chilled.

SUMMER

During midsummer barbeques are lit and potatoes boiled when people go out to their summer cottages to celebrate midsummer. New potatoes, fresh vegetables, pickled herring and other fish as well as steaks that melt in your mouth are the best of summer food and as a dessert, strawberries are, of course, the natural choice.

The saying "the Finnish summer is short and there's not much snow" is no longer true. Latterly the Scandinavian summers – at least in the form of warm weather - have been longer year by year. Mild August evenings are the perfect setting for instance for a crayfish party.

SUMMER APPETIZERS

If anything, pea soup is a traditional Finnish meal. Pea soup is often considered an everyday meal in Finland. But peas can also make a modern and festive appetizer. In this recipe this small green ball is turned into a delicacy of the 21st century. The bubbly, giving the pea soup a distinguished flavour, underlines the new way of serving of the soup at high society tables.

BUBBLY PEA SOUP

Boil the water and add one vegetable stock cube. Press the peas through a sieve or a thin towel. Add the pea purée and the bubbly to the vegetable broth. Let simmer for five minutes. Add the cream and salt. Bring to a boil. Taste for flavour. Whisk the soup bubbly with a hand held mixer.

500 G (17 OZ) FRESH OR FROZEN GREEN PEAS
600 ML (20 FL OZ) VEGETABLE STOCK
200 ML (6.8 FL OZ) SPARKLING WINE
100 ML (3.4 FL OZ) DOUBLE CREAM
SALT

Bubbly to bubblies! **Corodníu Non Plus Ultra Cuvée Reina Maria Cristina** *is an excellent companion to the fresh pea soup.*

Pickled herring and new potatoes are part of the Scandinavian summer as are grilled sausages and beer. In this recipe pickled herring and new potatoes are accompanied by a tartar of salmon and whitefish, and a perch carpaccio. A dip of dill in olive oil is an excellent seasoning. The fish of this appetizer are well-known to all Finns, but the way they are prepared and served is slightly more modern.

FISH TARTAR PLATTER

2 FILLETS OF PERCH
1 WHOLE PICKLED HERRING
200 G (7 OZ) SEA SALMON
200 G (7 OZ) WHITEFISH
2 SLICES OF RYE BREAD
2 TABLESPOONS CREAMY SOUR MILK (CRÈME FRAICHE)
1 BUNCH OF DILL
4 NEW POTATOES
1 TABLESPOON SMALL CAPERS
100 ML (3.4 FL OZ) OLIVE OIL
JUICE OF ½ LEMON

Wash and boil the potatoes. Leave to chill.

Fillet the pickled herring and skin both fillets. Remove the bones from the salmon and whitefish using tweezers. The bones are easily removed from the perch by dissecting them from the middle of the fillet with a knife. Cut the fish into small cubes.

Chop the potatoes into cubes the same size as the pickled herring. Mix capers, herring and potatoes. Chop the dill and add to the already mixed whitefish and salmon. Add the creamy sour milk, black pepper and salt. Stir.

Squeeze lemon juice over the perch and add a few drops of olive oil and a pinch of salt and white pepper. Cut the bread into cubes and mix with the perch.

Chop the dill and mix with olive oil. Serve with the fish tartar.

*Schnapps is the drink for Scandinavian cold fish dishes! We would choose **Skåne Akvavit,** a spicy spirit. Mineral water or even lager beer such as **Lapin Kulta IV** are also recommended, with or without the schnapps.*

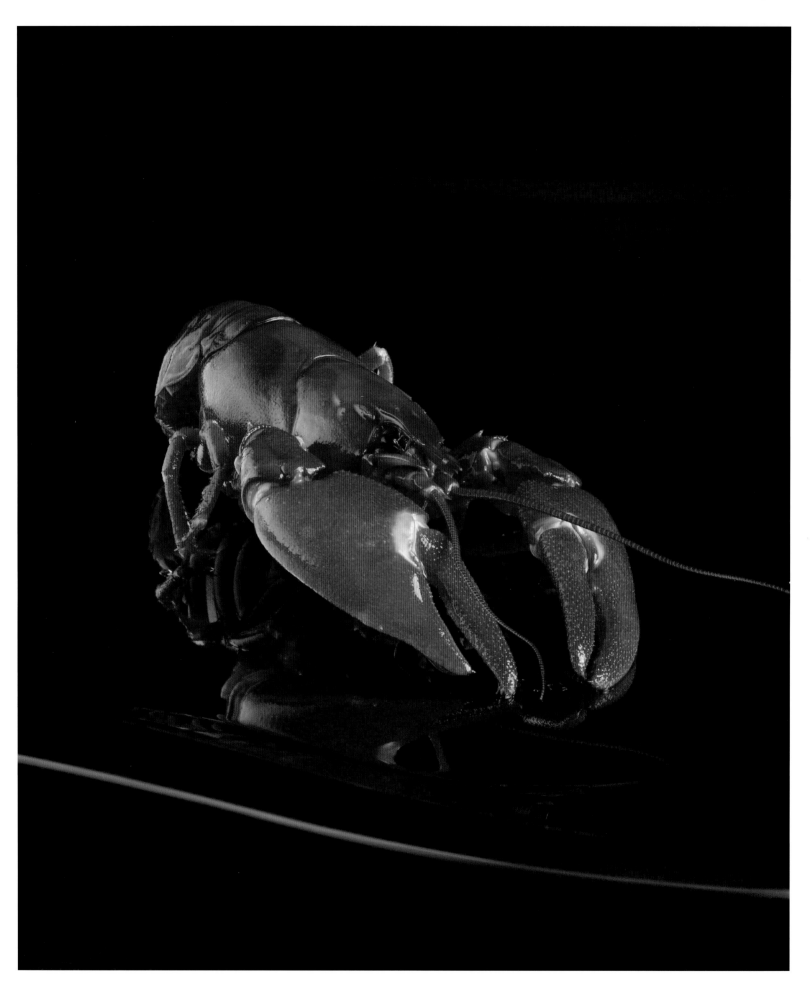

In Scandinavia, the latter part of summer is the time for crayfish parties. The crayfish are either enjoyed in the company of friends or at corporate dinners. All crayfish parties do not necessarily follow the old Finnish tradition to take a schnapps to every claw of crayfish one eats. Those who follow this tradition usually also follow the tradition to sing a drinking song to every schnapps.

There are two kinds of crayfish in the Finnish lakes: signal crayfish and European crayfish. Both taste delicious and their shell is soft enough for the diner not to have to use a chisel or a hammer to lay his hands on the delicious crayfish meat.

CRAYFISH

CHEESE SPREAD

CRAYFISH:
32 CRAYFISH (8 PER PERSON)
500 ML (17 FL OZ) WHITE WINE
4 LITRES (8.5 PT) WATER
DILL CROWNS
8 LUMPS OF SUGAR
180 G (6.3 OZ) SEA SALT

CHEESE SPREAD:
200 G (7 OZ) TUB OF NATURAL FRESH CHEESE
DILL
1 TEASPOON LEMON JUICE
2 TABLESPOONS CRAYFISH STOCK

Rinse the live crayfish. Boil the water and white wine in a big saucepan. Add the sugar, sea salt and half of the dill. Drop the crayfish into the boiling water. Boil for about 10 minutes. Remove the crayfish and dill and put them aside. Put the crayfish back into the stock once it has chilled. Add the unused stems of dill. Let the crayfish steep in the stock overnight or for at least 10 hours in order to enhance their flavour.

Mix the finely chopped dill, fresh cheese, lemon juice and broth. Serve with toast.

*A classic wine choice for crayfish is a white wine from the Sancerre region. **Pascal Jolivet Sancerre** has been a good choice throughout the years.*

SUMMER MAIN COURSES

Summer soup is a classic Finnish meal which is easy and quick to make. The ingredients you can pick in your own garden or buy at a local outdoor market. You will taste the excellence and freshness of summer soup by choosing fresh vegetables for ingredients. As the soup is partly made with milk it is somewhat sweet in taste. Thus there are people who like summer soup very much, and people who do not.

SUMMER SOUP

300 G (11 OZ) NEW POTATOES
200 G (7 OZ) CARROTS
200 G (7 OZ) CAULIFLOWER
200 ML (⅘ CUP) GREEN PEAS
100 ML (⅖ CUP) PARSLEY
500 ML (17 FL OZ) WATER
500 ML (17 FL OZ) MILK
1½ TABLESPOONS PLAIN WHEAT FLOUR
SALT
(1 VEGETABLE STOCK CUBE)
(1 TEASPOON BUTTER)

Boil the water. Add salt (or the vegetable stock cube). Wash and chop the vegetables. Put the carrots into the boiling water first. After about two minutes, add the potatoes and the peas. Add the cauliflower after another two minutes. Boil for about 10 more minutes. At this stage the vegetables will be only part boiled.

Mix flour and milk, pour the mix into a saucepan with the vegetables and stock. Leave to simmer until the vegetables are soft. If you do not use a vegetable stock cube you can add a tablespoon of butter making the soup slightly heavier. Taste for flavour. Sprinkle with lots of chopped parsley.

*Summer soup offers the tastes of Finnish summer at its best. A rosé wine goes perfectly with the soup. **Mateus Rosé** is an excellent drink for a warm summer's day.*

Fishermen are often heard debating which fish has the best flavour. Pike-perch almost always tops their list. And it's easy to agree; pike-perch is a topnotch fish! This recipe is ridiculously easy: catch a pike-perch, open a bottle of white wine, take a sip, also give the fish a sip, pour cream over the fish and leave it to cook in the oven for approximately an hour. Enjoy!

TOPNOTCH PIKE-PERCH

ONE PIKE-PERCH, 1½ KILOS (3.3 LB), CLEANED AND SCALED
300 ML (10 FL OZ) DOUBLE CREAM
1 SPRING ONION
DILL
150 ML (5 FL OZ) WHITE WINE
100 ML (3.4 FL OZ) MILK
100 ML (3.4 FL OZ) FISH STOCK
60 G (2 OZ) BUTTER
SALT
WHITE PEPPER

Chop the onion and fry lightly in butter. Set aside to cool. Chop the dill finely and mix with the onion in a few drops of white wine.

Rinse the pike-perch in cold water. Make two slashes lengthwise into the back of the fish. Place the fish on its belly in an ovenproof dish. Season with salt and white pepper. Put the mix of onion and dill into the slashes. Pour the rest of the white wine over the fish and cook it in the oven at 160 °C (320 °F) for 20 minutes.

Place a saucepan on low heat and put in the rest of the butter, the cream, fish stock and milk. Remove the fish from the oven and pour the creamy stock over it. Cook in the oven at 170 °C (340 °F) for another 50 minutes. Baste the fish with the stock every 15 minutes. Decorate with fresh dill. Serve with new potatoes.

*Chardonnay white wines go excellently with slightly creamy fish dishes. A good choice is **Chilean Caliterra Chardonnay Reserva.***

Vorschmack is originally a dish from central and eastern Europe. It found its way into the hearts and onto the dining tables of Finns having been introduced to them by the Finnish war hero, Marshal Mannerheim. It is known that Mannerheim, who was recently chosen to be the most important Finn of all time, considered Vorschmack to be his favourite dish. He always had his Vorschmack with a spiced schnapps which was later to become well-known as the "Marshal's schnapps".

VORSCHMACK

POTATO SALAD, BEETROOT CRISPS

Remove the membranes and the fat from the lamb and the beef. Chop the meat into pieces the size of the tip of your thumb. Put the pieces of meat on a baking tray and roast them and the chopped onions in the oven at 200 °C (390 °F) for approximately 10 minutes. Leave the meat to cool and put the two kinds of meat together with the garlic, the herring and the fillets of anchovy through a mincer until they resemble a coarse pate.

Mix the tomato purée, beef stock and freshly ground white pepper with the pate. Pour the mixture into a casserole dish and cook in the oven at 150 °C (300 °F) for at least 4 hours. Check that the pate does not dry while in the oven. Add beef stock, if necessary.

Boil the potatoes. Leave them to cool and peel them. Chop the potatoes and the pickled cucumbers into dice-sized pieces. Mix them together and add the sour cream "smetana". Serve the potato salad with honey.

Wash the beetroots and cut them wafer thin using a cheese slicer. Pour oil into a small saucepan and heat until it is very hot. Put the slices of beetroot into the hot oil and leave to cook for a minute or two. Remove the slices from the oil using

VORSCHMACK:
1 KG (2.2 LB) BONE-FREE LAMB
200 G (7 OZ) BEEF, E.G. SILVERSIDE
50 G (1.8 OZ) PICKLED HERRING
50 G (1.8 OZ) FILLETS OF ANCHOVY
2 LARGE ONIONS
300 ML (10 FL OZ) BEEF STOCK
100 ML (3.4 FL OZ) TOMATO PURÉE
3 GARLIC CLOVES
WHITE PEPPER

POTATO SALAD:
400 G (14 OZ) FIRM POTATOES
200 G (7 OZ) RUSSIAN-STYLE PICKLED CUCUMBER
20 ML (0.7 FL OZ) RUSSIAN STYLE SOUR CREAM "SMETANA"
CLEAR HONEY

BEETROOT CRISPS:
2 MEDIUM-SIZED BEETROOTS
20 ML (0.7 FL OZ) COOKING OIL

a perforated ladle or a sieve and leave to dry on a kitchen towel. Serve with the Vorschmack and the potato salad.

*In this recipe we have been true to Marshal Mannerheim's tradition and recommend you to enjoy your Vorschmack complemented by the **Marshal's schnapps** or another high quality vodka. A chilled lager such as **Karjala III** or a glass of red wine are also excellent companions of Vorschmack.*

Around 20th August you will hear gunshots galore in the lake districts of Finland. The hunting season for mallard is the culmination of late summer and indicates the starting point for the hunting season of many kinds of game. Not only fishing but hunting, too, is an ancient Finnish pastime – and people even made a living of it to the enjoyment of master and dog.

Mallard is a delicacy of late summer which is easy to make when you simmer it in a pot in red wine.

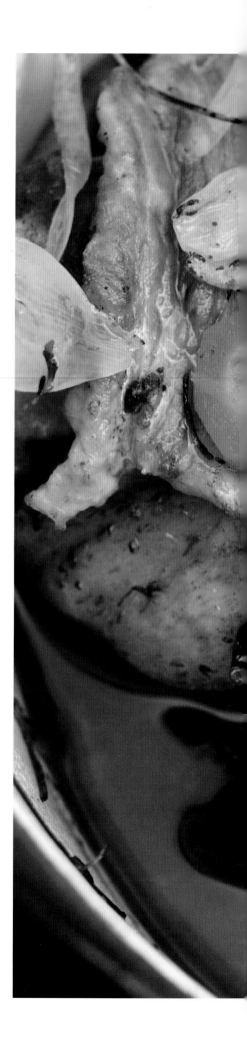

POT-ROASTED MALLARD

GARLIC POTATOES

One mallard will serve two or maximum three persons. For a bigger group you need more than one mallard.

Rinse the mallard in cold water. Fry until brown on each side. Sprinkle salt and freshly ground allspice berries on the mallard. Peel and chop the vegetables. Fry the vegetables, herbs and spices lightly in butter in the pot, preferably made of cast iron. Put the mallard into the pot and the slices of pork on top. Pour the wine into the pot and add a pinch of salt. Leave to simmer under cover for about 1 hour 15 minutes.

Peel and halve the potatoes lengthwise. Cut a few slashes into the potato on the top side. Crush the garlic cloves and rosemary and mix with the butter. Ladle lots of garlic butter on the potatoes and add a pinch of salt. Bake in the oven at 170 °C (340 °F) for approximately 55 minutes.

Chill the mallard stock and skim the fat off the top. Heat again and serve as gravy.

Tip: You can add a bit of cream to the stock for a milder flavour. The special taste of mallard will not be too strong if you remove the skin before cooking.

SERVES TWO:
1 PLUCKED, CLEANED MALLARD
150 G (5.3 OZ) PORK BELLY OR BACON
3 CARROTS
2 ONIONS
5 GARLIC CLOVES
ROSEMARY
THYME
3 DRIED ALLSPICE BERRIES
4 JUNIPER BERRIES
1 BAY LEAF
300 ML (10 FL OZ) RED WINE
1 TABLESPOON BUTTER
SALT
BLACK PEPPER CORNS

GARLIC POTATOES:
1 KG (2.2 LB) POTATOES
3 GARLIC CLOVES
80 G (2.8 OZ) BUTTER
ROSEMARY
SALT

*Mallard and Pinot Noir is a classic combination, but if you are lucky enough to get a wild mallard a good Chianti is an even better choice. **Villa Cafaggio Chianti Classico** is excellent, year after year.*

Caesar salad or more exactly Caesar dressing was invented in the American cuisine and has been a world-wide success. Salads drizzled with this dressing are served today in almost every part of the world. In this version the delicious global taste is combined with ingredients from the Finnish archipelago. The salad gets a special touch from the crôutes of black Åland bread.

CAESAR SALAD ARCHIPELAGO STYLE

SALAD:
2–3 DIFFERENT KINDS OF LETTUCE
1 BOX OF CHERRY TOMATOES
300 G (11 OZ) SMALL SMOKED VENDACE
300 G (11 OZ) SMOKED SALMON
½ BLACK BREAD FROM ÅLAND
1 TEASPOON BUTTER

DRESSING:
1 TIN OF ANCHOVY
200 ML (6.8 FL OZ) MAYONNAISE
100 ML (3.4 FL OZ) DOUBLE CREAM
1–2 TEASPOONS DIJON MUSTARD
JUICE OF ½ LEMON
100 G (3.5 OZ) PARMESAN CHEESE

Smoke the fish e.g. in smoking bags in the oven – each kind in its own one. Ready-smoked fish is also a good alternative.

Finely chop 4–7 fillets of anchovy. The number of anchovies influence the saltiness of the gravy. Squeeze the lemon juice. Mix mayonnaise, cream, anchovy, lemon juice and mustard. Taste.

Wash the lettuce and tomatoes. Shred the lettuce into a bowl. Cut the tomatoes in halves and mix with the lettuce. Add the whole vendace and the salmon cut into bits. Cut the bread into 2 cm (1 inch) long pieces and fry in butter until crispy. Leave to chill and place on top of the salad together with parmesan cheese.

Tip: The dressing can be mixed with the salad or served separately.

*This dish is a wonderful mix of fresh archipelago flavors. **Keisari Lager** has a crisp bitterness that matches beautifully the flavors of the dish.*

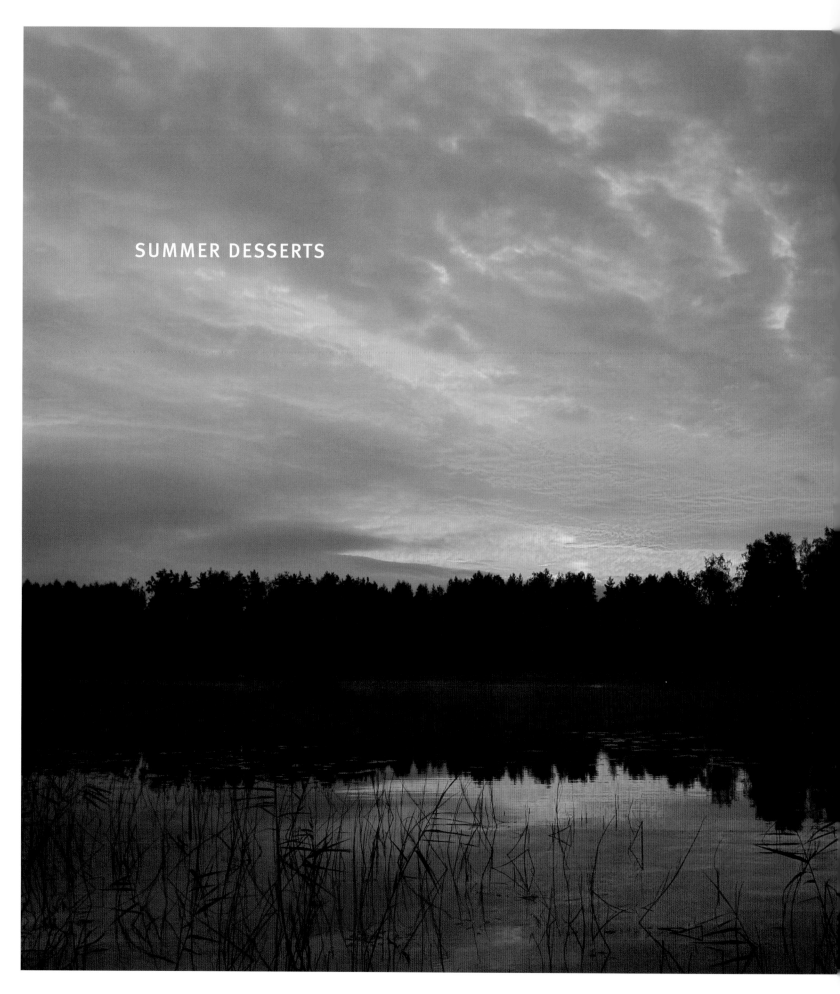

SUMMER DESSERTS

Strawberry meringue is the dessert for summer. It is superbly delicious made of freshly picked strawberries. If you want the kids not to leave the dinner table after the main course, serve this sweet and fresh strawberry meringue as a dessert.

STRAWBERRY MERINGUE

MERINGUE:
4 EGG WHITES
200 ML (⅘ CUP) SUGAR

FOR DECORATION:
2 LITRES (8.4 CUPS) STRAWBERRIES
200 ML (6.8 FL OZ) DOUBLE CREAM
1 TEASPOON SUGAR

Separate egg yolks and whites. Pour a quarter of the sugar into a bowl and add the egg whites. Beat into a hard foam and add the rest of the sugar little by little. Pipe on baking paper into two separate discs, diameter approx. 20 cm (8 inches). Bake in the oven for approx. two hours in 120 °C (250 °F) until crispy. Leave to cool in the oven.

Whip the cream and add the sugar. Spread the whipped cream on one of the meringue discs. Add whole hulled strawberries. Place the second meringue disc on the strawberries and spread whipped cream. Decorate with halved strawberries and edible flowers.

Tip: If you want to save time, you can substitute the home-made meringue bases with ready-made ones. You can also colour the cream pale pink by adding a little strawberry juice to the whipped cream.

*A Strawberry Cider is the right choice for this superb summer dessert. **Olvi's Fizz Strawberry Cooler** has a hint of vanilla in it. The combination of strawberry and vanilla flavors bring into mind vanilla ice cream with strawberry jam complimenting well the tastes of Strawberry Meringue.*

In this recipe the sweet and sour lemon and lime sorbet and the salty sal ammoniac sauce shake hands like brothers. The sorbet is at its best as a refreshener on a hot summer's day.

Sal ammoniac is not very well-known outside the Scandinavian countries. It is often mistaken for its sweeter and soft brother, liquorice. As a matter of fact, one should not at all speak about sweetness of taste when talking about sal ammoniac, as in fact it is salty. This makes sal ammoniac taste a bit peculiar to people who are not used to it. On the other hand, there are many people who have tasted no other goodies having got used to its taste.

LEMON AND LIME SORBET

SAL AMMONIAC SAUCE

SORBET:
4 LIMES
4 LEMONS
100 ML (⅖ CUP) SUGAR
2 TABLESPOONS LIMONCELLO
2 EGG WHITES

SAL AMMONIAC SAUCE:
80 G (2.8 OZ) E.G. SAL AMMONIAC SQUARES
50 G (1.8 OZ) SOFT LIQUORICE
100–200 ML (3.4–6.8 FL OZ) WATER

Cut the limes and lemons into halves and squeeze the juice. Pour the juice into a saucepan and heat. Add sugar and Limoncello. Set aside and pour into a metal bowl. Leave to chill.

Whip the egg whites into a foam and add to the lemon/lime mixture. Stir well. Put into the freezer. Stir the sorbet every 20 minutes until it starts to freeze. Remove the sorbet from the freezer just before serving.

Pour 100 ml (3.4 fl oz) water into a small saucepan. Cut the sal ammoniac squares and liquorice into small pieces with a sharp knife and melt in the saucepan on medium heat. Stir every couple of minutes. Do not let the sauce thicken too much. Add water, if necessary. When the consistency of the sauce is a bit like syrup but still runny, put aside to cool. Serve with the lime and lemon sorbet.

Cugnexio Moscato d'Asti, a bubbly sweet wine from northern Italy, is a perfect companion to this fresh, salty dessert.

Beestings is the milk that is drawn from a cow directly after calving. The vitamins, trace elements and above all the rich proteins are of utmost importance to the new-born calf for its early growth. No wonder beestings, which enhances muscle growth, has become popular among body-builders.

Beestings brulé is a delicious and healthy dessert. The cinnamon, burned sugar and slightly sour berries complement the beestings, which has set in the oven.

BEESTINGS BRULÉ

800 ML (27 FL OZ) BEESTINGS
2 TABLESPOONS RAW SUGAR
50 ML (3 TABLESPOONS) CINNAMON
BERRIES

Pour the beestings into a serving bowl/individual serving bowls. Bake in the oven for approximately 25–30 minutes. Leave to cool and sprinkle a thin layer of cinnamon over it. Sprinkle some raw sugar on top. Burn the surface brown with a blowtorch or in the oven under a grill. Decorate with raspberries or other berries.

*Beestings gives this dessert quite a strong flavour and thus the wine can also be rich in taste. **Sweet Chilean Torres Vendima Tardía Riesling** is an excellent wine and together with this brulé they make a fabulous pair.*

AUTUMN

In the autumn, the summer's harvest is gathered in fields and gardens as well as in the forests. The gifts of autumn are vegetables, root vegetables, berries and mushrooms. Game like moose, deer and fowl bring exotic and strong flavours to seasonal dishes as the autumn evenings are drawing in.

AUTUMN APPETIZERS

Cep is a highly appreciated mushroom e.g. in Italy and the Scandinavian countries export tons of it to Italy every year. However, there is space for new "cep entrepreneurs" because people say that in the Finnish forests alone ceps worth millions of Euros rot every year. The core of the problem is, however, the difficulty in finding the cep; usually less than ten per cent of the estimated total is harvested from the forests. But even this gives enough mushrooms to make thousands of tasty cep pies and other cep delicacies.

CEP PIE

Rub the butter, flour and porridge oats into a smooth paste. Mix the baking powder, salt and water. Knead, and line an ovenproof pastry dish. Bake blind in the oven at in 150 °C (300 °F) for about 10 minutes.

    Fry the ceps lightly in a frying pan. Add the chopped onion, parsley and bacon. Season with black pepper. Fry until the bacon is crispy. Spread the ceps-bacon mix evenly on the pre-baked pastry case. Mix the eggs, creamy sour milk and milk. Pour the mixture on top of the layer of ceps and bacon. Bake in the oven at 170 °C (340 °F) for about 20 minutes until the filling has set.

Cep pie needs a strong white wine, for example a
Condrieu Les Vins de Vienne.

PIE CRUST:
150 ML (⅗ CUP) PLAIN WHEAT FLOUR
150 ML (⅗ CUP) PORRIDGE OATS
100 G (3.5 OZ) BUTTER
1 TEASPOON BAKING POWDER
100 ML (3.4 FL OZ) WATER
½ TEASPOON SALT

FILLING:
300–400 ML (1 ¼–1 ⅝) CLEANED,
CHOPPED CEPS (BOLETUS EDULIS)
150 G (5.3 OZ) SMOKED STREAKY BACON
1 LARGE ONION
PARSLEY
2 EGGS
100 ML (3.4 FL OZ) CREAMY SOUR MILK
100 ML (3.4 FL OZ) MILK
BLACK PEPPER CORNS

Opinions about the taste of liver is split. Not everyone likes it. Even if you have not been a lover of liver before, this recipe is worth trying. The sherry softens the strong taste of the liver and gives the liver bake a splendidly sweetish flavour. To friends of liver this recipe opens up a new world: the flavours of sherry and raisins melt together but do not draw too much attention from the main ingredient.

LIVER AND SHERRY BAKE

Boil the rice in the milk. Remove the membrane from the liver and mince the liver, mix it with onions fried lightly in butter, the beaten egg, the sherry and the raisins. Mix thoroughly. Pour into an oven-proof dish. Cook in the oven at 160 °C (320 °F) for 70 minutes. Serve with fresh cranberries dusted with icing sugar.

Liver bake, seasoned with sherry to make it more modern, does not necessarily require an accompanying wine.
Cold milk *is a straight-forward and correct choice.*

500 G (18 OZ/1.1 LB) OX OR CALF'S LIVER
150 G (5.3 OZ) PUDDING RICE
700 ML (24 FL OZ) MILK
1 ONION
1 EGG
1 TABLESPOON BUTTER
100 ML (⅖ CUP) RAISINS
50 ML (1.7 FL OZ) SHERRY
MAJORAM
WHITE PEPPER
SALT
3 TABLESPOONS TREACLE

The mild lemon-flavoured carpaccio and the sweet and sour raspberry vinaigrette is an exotic and delicate combination. With a bit of effort you can make this dish extremely attractive and impressive. You may choose to decorate the plate with edible flowers and fresh raspberries.

REINDEER CARPACCIO

RASPBERRY VINAIGRETTE

Remove the membranes from the reindeer fillet and wrap it tightly in cling film to make a cylinder shaped roll. Put it into the freezer and let it freeze for approximately two hours. The meat is ready to be cut when it is slightly frozen all through and can easily be cut into wafer thin slices with a knife.

Make the raspberry vinaigrette while the meat is in the freezer. You can also make it earlier and marinate the asparagus and the onions in the vinaigrette overnight.

Purée a quarter of the raspberries. Save the rest of the berries for decoration. Pour the purée into a small saucepan, add the water, the raspberry liqueur, the vinegar and the sugar. Stir well. Let the vinaigrette simmer for a while.

Wash and chop the asparagus and the onions into pieces to the size of the tip of your little finger. Pour a little water into a saucepan and steam the vegetables in a strainer above boiling water for a couple of minutes.

If you want the vinaigrette to be somewhat thicker, put half a sheet of gelatin into the boiling mixture. Put the vegetables into the vinaigrette. Remove the fillet of reindeer from the freezer. Also remove the cling film. Cut the fillet into wafer thin slices and place them on a plate. Squeeze some lemon juice and sprinkle some olive oil, some freshly ground black pepper and a pinch of flake salt over the slices.

REINDEER CARPACCIO:
1 OUTER FILLET OF REINDEER
1 LEMON
OLIVE OIL
FRESH GROUND BLACK PEPPER
SALT

RASPBERRY VINAIGRETTE:
100 G (3.5 OZ) RASPBERRIES
1 SPRING ONION
1 TOMATO
100 G MINI ASPARGUS
4 TABLESPOONS RASPBERRY LIQUEUR
50 ML (1.7 FL OZ) WATER
1 TABLESPOON SUGAR
1 TABLESPOON RED WINE VINEGAR
(½ SHEET OF GELATIN)

A fillet of reindeer is a superb game product which is guaranteed tomake a dinner very special, even festive. This should also be evident in the choice of wine. **Marguerite Carillon Volnay 1er Cru Les Santenots** *is a versatile wine and its acidity, typical of pinot noir, is an extremely suitable companion to the reindeer carpaccio with a hint of raspberry flavour.*

In this simple soup two traditional Finnish delicacies from rural tables are combined: moose meat and oven-baked cheese. If you manage to get ready-made oven-baked cheese this recipe does not require very good culinary skills: shoot a moose out of the freezer, cook, cut the ready-made oven-baked cheese and put into the stock. Therefore this soup can be recommended also for hunters who are not used to create a dinner of what they have hunted.

SOUP OF MOOSE AND OVEN-BAKED CHEESE

Mix the lukewarm milk, the cheese rennet and the salt. Leave to rest under cover for 25 minutes. Cut crosses in the cheese substance with a knife. Leave to rest for a short while. Put the cheese substance into a dish. Do not stir. Bake in the oven at 250 °C (480 °F) until the surface gets brown spots. As the cheese is baking, large amounts of whey will spill from the cheese, so it is wise to place a baking tray under the dish.

Rinse and dry the meat. Season with herbs, salt and pepper. Place the slices of bacon round the meat. Roast in the oven at 200 °C (390 °F) for about 20 minutes. Take the meat from the oven, remove the bacon and herbs. Place the meat in the stock which should be at boiling point and seasoned with bay leaves. Do not allow it boil. Leave the meat to cook for another 35 minutes. Remove the meat and cut into thin slices. Sieve the stock through a linen towel to make it as clear as possible. Put the slices of roast and pieces of the oven-baked cheese into the stock. Decorate with parsley.

SOUP OF MOOSE:
800 G (28 OZ/1.8 LB) PIECE OF MOOSE, E.G. TOPSIDE
3 SLICES OF STREAKY BACON
A TWIG OF ROSEMARY
THYME
SALT
BLACK PEPPER CORNS
500 G (18 OZ/1.1 LB) OVEN-BAKED CHEESE (READY-MADE OR HOME MADE)
700 ML (24 FL OZ) BEEF STOCK
2 BAY LEAVES

OVEN-BAKED CHEESE:
4 LITERS (8.4 PT) FULL CREAM MILK
1 DESSERT SPOON CHEESE RENNET
1 TEASPOON SALT

*Finnish-Scandinavian soups are challenging to traditional wines, Surprisingly the recommended drink is the delicious Finnish home-brewed beer **"Sahti"**.*

AUTUMN MAIN COURSES

Loin of pork is well known to most people. However, the way to prepare it has been very dull in most countries: the pre-seasoned loin is taken from its vacuum pack and grilled.

This recipe proves that the loin of pork, complemented by suitable extras, will make an exquisite dish even for a elegant dinner.

LOIN OF PORK

CAULIFLOWER PURÉE, DARK BEER GRAVY

1 KG (2.2 LB) LOIN OF PORK
SALT
PEPPER

BEER GRAVY:
0.33 LITER (11 FL OZ) DARK BEER
300 ML (10 FL OZ) BEEF STOCK
100 ML (3.4 FL OZ) TREACLE
2 CARROTS
1 ONION
1 BAY LEAF
3 DRIED ALLSPICE BERRIES
FRESH THYME
2 TABLESPOONS CORNFLOUR
(OR SIMILAR THICKENING FLOUR)
SALT

CAULIFLOWER PURÉE:
1 CAULIFLOWER
3 FLOURY POTATOES (E.G. VAN GOGH)
50 G (1.8 OZ) PARMESAN CHEESE,
FRESHLY GROUND
200 ML (7 FL OZ) MILK
1 TABLESPOON BUTTER

Rinse the pork and dry with kitchen towels. Fry in a frying pan until brown and season. Transfer the pork into an ovenproof dish and bake at 180 °C (360 °F) until the inner temperature of the meat is 79 °C (174 °F).

Peel and chop the vegetables. Add them and the spices to the simmering stock. Add the beer and the treacle. Let boil for approximately an hour. Strain, put back on the stove and thicken the gravy with cornflour.

Peel the potatoes and wash the cauliflower. Boil both until soft. Mash the potatoes. Add the warm milk, butter and grated cheese. Mix well. Cream the cauliflower using a hand mixer. Mix the mash and the cauliflower purée. Add salt.

*The Ripasso wines from the area of Valpolicello in Italy are sufficiently acidy and rich to accompany pork. **Tommasi** is a vineyard to be trusted and their **Ripasso** goes excellently with this dish.*

This is a more elegant version of stuffed cabbage and beef olives! Usually a mix of minced beef and rice is used as filling in cabbage rolls. This recipe makes an exotic exception: instead of minced beef and rice the cabbage leaf is wrapped around inner fillet of deer. The white cabbage is replaced by its more elegant French cousin, Savoy cabbage, which also grows as far north as in Scandinavia.

DEER AND CABBAGE OLIVES

TREACLE GRAVY, LINGONBERRY JELLY

Pour the water into a saucepan and boil the lingonberries for about five minutes. Add sugar. Set aside and mash the berries with a potato masher. Strain the juice and set aside. Soak the sheets of gelatin in cold water for five minutes. Squeeze them dry and put them in a saucepan with about 50 ml (1.7 fl oz) boiling water. Remove the saucepan from the heat and stir until the gelatin has melted. Pour the gelatin into the lingonberry juice, mix and leave to set in the fridge for an hour. Cut into small cubes just before serving.

Put the cabbage into a saucepan with boiling water. Remove the outer cabbage leaves as soon as they go soft. Please note that Savoy cabbage softens much more quickly than ordinary white cabbage. The Savoy cabbage is more porous and thus the water can soften also the inner layers quickly.

Brown the whole fillet of deer in a cast iron frying pan. Cut it into approximately 5 cm (2 inch) thick pieces. Season with fresh majoram, salt and black pepper. Roll a cabbage leaf round the piece of fillet and place in an ovenproof dish. Pour treacle on each "package". Roast in the oven at 130 °C (270 F°) for approximately 20 minutes.

Put a stock cube into boiling water. Add the bay leaf, the pepper and the chopped vegetables. Simmer for approximately 30 minutes. Strain the stock and put it back on the stove. Add treacle and Amaretto. Bring to the boil. Taste for flavour. Boiled potatoes or Parisian potatoes go well with this dish.

*Elegant game combined with the sweet taste of the cabbage cries out for a good red wine. Such a one is e.g. **Pio Cesare Barbera d'Alban**.*

LINGONBERRY JELLY:
200 G (7 OZ) LINGONBERRIES
300 ML (10 FL OZ) WATER
1 TEASPOON SUGAR
3 SHEETS OF GELATIN

DEER AND CABBAGE OLIVES:
500 G (18 OZ/1.1 LB) INNER FILLET OF DEER
1 SAVOY CABBAGE
FRESH MAJORAM
TREACLE
BLACK PEPPER CORNS
SALT
WATER

TREACLE GRAVY:
400 ML (13.5 FL OZ) BEEF STOCK
100 ML (3.4 FL OZ) TREACLE
2 TABLESPOONS AMARETTO LIQUEUR
THE STOCK OF THE DEER OLIVES
1 CARROT
1 ONION
3 DRIED ALLSPICE BERRIES
1 DRIED BAY LEAF
CORNFLOUR (OR SIMILAR THICKENING FLOUR)

What a filling supper for gentlemen! Who said that a sandwich will leave you hungry? The recipe is easy and tasty. Even unskilled cooks can fix this. The salty bacon and pork fillet will melt in your mouth together with the full-flavored chanterelle gravy. The soft red wine will complement the aftertaste.

HUNTER'S SANDWICH

Cut four steaks out of the fillet of pork. Club the meat lightly. Fry the mushrooms lightly in a frying pan until their natural moisture has evaporated. Add some butter and the finely-chopped onion. Fry for a while and add the flour stirring constantly. Pour the cream and stock over and let it thicken into a thickish gravy. Add salt.

Fry the steaks in the frying pan. Add salt and black pepper. The slices of pork can be fried in a frying pan or baked in the oven. If you choose the latter, about 3 minutes in 200 °C (400 °F) in the oven under grill is enough.

Build the sandwich: grill the slices of bacon. Place them on a slice of bread, then the meat and top it with lots of chanterelle gravy. Give it a fresh taste and pretty look with fine-cut parsley.

*To the gentle, smooth, rounded taste of this hunter's sandwich you may want to choose a light, fruity red wine, for instance **Douhin Moulin-à-Vent.***

500 G (18 OZ/1.1 LB) OUTER FILLET OF PORK
1 PACKET/150 G (5.3 OZ) OF SMOKED STREAKY BACON
1 LITRE (8.4 CUPS) OF CHANTERELLES
1 ONION
1 TABLESPOON BUTTER
200 ML (6.8 FL OZ) DOUBLE CREAM
100 ML (3.4 FL OZ) BEEF STOCK
1 MULTI-GRAIN LOAF OF BREAD
1 TABLESPOON PLAIN WHEAT FLOUR FOR THICKENING
PARSLEY
SALT
BLACK PEPPER

LOIN OF LAMB

BARLEY RISOTTO, BEER GRAVY

In this recipe the present and the past meet. Grains of barley are part of a centuries old Finnish traditional cuisine. Little by little the softer and quicker-to-boil rice took the place of the barley. The story is similar to that of the turnip and the potato that made its way to Europe from America.

The present time in this recipe is represented by the way the grains of barley are prepared. In recipes similar to that of Italian risotto, Finnish grains of barley are put into a bath of white wine. They get an exquisite flavour of the chanterelles and hide under a veil of grated parmesan cheese.

MUTTON:
2 WHOLE RACKS OF LAMB
(ABOUT 1 KILO [2.2 LB] IN ALL)
200 ML (6.8 FL OZ) LAGER
FRESH THYME
FRESH ROSEMARY
1 TEASPOON SUGAR
BLACK PEPPER CORNS

BARLEY RISOTTO:
400 ML (1 ⅝ CUPS) GRAINS OF BARLEY
1 LITRE (8.4 CUPS) CHANTERELLES
1 ONION
50 ML (1.7 FL OZ) COOKING OIL
400 ML (13.5 FL OZ) VEGETABLE OR LAMB STOCK
200 ML (6.8 FL OZ) WHITE WINE
4 TABLESPOONS GRATED PARMESAN CHEESE
SALT
2 TABLESPOONS CREAM

BEER GRAVY:
300 ML (10 FL OZ) LAGER
400 ML (13.5 FL OZ) BEEF STOCK OR LAMB STOCK
SOME OF THE ROASTED LAMB JUICES
1 ONION
3 GARLIC CLOVES
1 CARROT
1 TEASPOON SUGAR
FRESH THYME
1 BAY LEAF
2–3 WHOLE DRIED ALLSPICE BERRIES
2 TABLESPOONS CORNFLOUR
3 TABLESPOONS BEER TO THICKEN

Mix the lager, chopped herbs, sugar and black pepper. Put the whole racks of lamb to marinate in the mix. Leave overnight.

Wash, peel and chop the vegetables. Pour the stock and the beer into a saucepan. Add the chopped vegetables and spices. Let the gravy simmer for approximately 90 minutes. If there is fluid left after cooking the racks, pour a few drops of it into the gravy to add flavour. Strain the gravy and thicken with a mix of cornflour and lager.

Remove the lamb from the marinade and pat it dry with kitchen towels. Put it in an ovenproof dish or on a baking tray. Sprinkle salt on the lamb. Roast in the oven at 200 °C (390 °F) for approximately 25 minutes. Carve the rack into separate chops and serve.

Wash the chanterelles. Chop and fry lightly in a frying pan until their natural moisture has evaporated. Set aside.

Heat the oil in a saucepan. Add the chopped onion and cook until pale golden. Pour the grains of barley into the saucepan, mix with the onion and cook for a couple of minutes. Add the white wine and cook until the wine has evaporated. Pour the lamb or beef stock, 200 ml (6.8 fl oz) at a time, over the barley and simmer until the broth has evaporated. Repeat until the grains of barley are al dente. Add the chanterelles, cream, grated parmesan cheese and salt – in this order. Taste for flavour.

*A good companion to the herb-flavoured lamb must be a herb-flavoured wine. We suggest a red wine, preferably **Pichon Lonqueville Comtesse de Lalande Réserve de la Comtesse.***

REINDEER WITH CLOUDBERRIES

POTATOES WITH HERBS

Peel the potatoes. Pour the water into a saucepan and boil the potatoes. Do not let them go mushy. Drain the water from the saucepan and set the potatoes aside for a moment.

Finely chop the sage, parsley, thyme and garlic cloves. Put the herbs into a large dish with a rounded base. Add some black pepper from the mill.

Pour the water into a saucepan and add a stock cube. Add the chopped vegetables, half of the cloudberries, a couple of twigs of thyme, allspice berries, the bay leaf and the cloudberry liqueur to the clear broth. Boil slowly for about an hour. Sieve and thicken with cornflour. Boil until the gravy thickens. You can pour liquid from cooking the reindeer into the gravy.

Rinse the fillets of reindeer in cold water. Dry them and brown in butter in a cast iron frying pan until the surface of the meat is brown. Season with salt and black pepper. Wrap the fillet in foil and roast in the oven at 200 °C (390 °F) approximately 5 minutes.

Pour the cooking oil into a saucepan and heat. The oil is hot enough when it starts boiling when you put in a potato. Deep fry the potatoes in oil for approximately 4 minutes. Lift them out with a perforated ladle or a sieve into the dish with the herbs. Roll the potatoes carefully in the herbs and add salt.

MEAT:
700 G (25 OZ/1.5 LB) OUTER FILLET OF REINDEER (2 FILLETS)
1 TEASPOON BUTTER
SALT
BLACK PEPPER CORNS

GRAVY:
100 G (3.5 OZ) CLOUDBERRIES
50 ML (1.7 FL OZ) CLOUDBERRY LIQUEUR
500 ML (17 FL OZ) CLEAR STOCK
1 ONION
1 CARROT
FRESH THYME
2–3 DRIED ALLSPICE BERRIES
1 BAY LEAF
2–3 TABLESPOONS CORNFLOUR (OR SIMILAR THICKENING FLOUR)

POTATOES WITH HERBS:
800 G (28 OZ/1.8 LB) POTATOES
1 LITRE (2.1 PT) WATER
PARSLEY
SAGE
THYME
2–3 GARLIC CLOVES
500 ML (17 FL OZ) COOKING OIL
BLACK PEPPER CORNS
SALT

Shiraz wines are spicy enough to suit the strong flavour of reindeer. Australia is well-known for its Shiraz wines. **Wyndham Estate Shiraz** *is both spicy and fruity.*

Sautéed reindeer is probably the most well-known dish of reindeer meat. Served with mash it is excellent, but as it is the most often served dish of reindeer other reindeer dishes have almost been forgotten. This is a pity, because both the outer and the inner fillets of reindeer are just delicious.

Despite the fact that more than 200,000 reindeer graze in the northern parts of Finland, reindeer delicacies are not seen every day on dinner plates in Finland. This is partly due to the fact that you can buy fresh reindeer only during a few weeks after the rounding up and separating of reindeer herds. On the other hand, the availability of frozen reindeer meat is already much better these days, and the flavour of frozen reindeer meat is almost as delicious as that of fresh reindeer meat. Fillet of reindeer with cloudberry gravy takes the diner to the exotic atmosphere of Lapland.

AUTUMN DESSERTS

Sour full cream milk is a sour milk product which is not very well known outside the Scandinavian countries. It looks a bit like yoghurt. The texture of sour full cream milk is different – it is thicker and the taste is also very different.

As long as you have milk you can make new sour full cream milk. You need only to save a little bit of "viili" to use as a "root" in the making of new sour full cream milk.

SOUR FULL CREAM MILK "VIILI"

ROSE-HIP COMPOTE

SOUR FULL CREAM MILK, "VIILI":
200 ML (6.8 FL OZ) SOUR FULL CREAM MILK
1 LITRE (2.1 PT) MILK

ROSE-HIP COMPOTE:
500 ML (2 ⅛ CUPS) RIPE FRESH ROSE-HIPS
GRANULATED SUGAR
WATER

Spoon the sour full cream milk into a dish. Add the milk and leave to rest for 24 hours in a non-draughty place in room temperature, where it will set.

Pick half a liter (2 cups) light or bright red rose-hips from your neighbor's rose bushes. Do not choose over-ripe dark red berries. Halve the berries and remove the seeds carefully e.g. with the handle of a teaspoon. Put the cleaned rose-hips into a saucepan and pour water to cover the rose-hips.

Boil on low temperature for 30 minutes. Press the rose-hips through a sieve. Add sugar, and half the amount of the rose-hip jam. Let cool and serve with the set sour full cream milk.

Tip: if stealing rose-hips from your neighbour's rose bushes, cleaning and cooking the rose-hips feels too much of a bother, you can with a good conscience use ready-made jam. You will find it in well stocked health food shops.

Whipped lingonberry porridge is a good example of how in Finland, which used to be a poor country some 100 years ago, one learned to make good food out of few and simple ingredients. Whipped lingonberry porridge has not become old-fashioned. It is still one of children's favourites, although the industrial revolution has filled the shelves of the food stores with desserts and puddings, one sweeter and more colourful than the other.

WHIPPED LINGONBERRY PORRIDGE

1.2 LITRES (2.5 PT) WATER
400 ML (1 ⅝ CUPS) LINGONBERRIES
100 ML (⅖ CUP) SUGAR
150 ML (⅗ CUP) SEMOLINA

Cook the lingonberries for approximately 15 minutes in boiling water. Set aside and crush the berries with e.g. a pestle. Strain the mixture using a fine mesh sieve and save the juice. Put the juice back on the heat and add the sugar. When the juice starts to boil, pour in the semolina stirring constantly. Boil for approximately 10 minutes or until the porridge is thick enough. Let cool for a while and whisk until fluffy using a hand held mixer. If the porridge is too sour add sugar according to taste. Serve with milk and sugar.

The flavour of the lingonberry needs a wine which is very sweet. You could, for instance, serve a glass of **Ruffino Serelle,** *a dessert wine from Tuscany.*

WINTER

In the winter the Finnish nature rests and gathers strength for the coming spring. In the north it is very cold and dark for most of the day. An outsider might think that the inhabitants of the far north are hibernating. But first impressions are deceptive as, for instance, in December Finland is buzzing with people preparing for the big celebration at Christmas.

In February-March, when the sun gives a promise of spring, the Finns take out their skies, skates and jigging equipment and go out on the frozen lakes. After a day's outing hot soup, berries and a candle-lit dinner will do wonders for body and soul.

WINTER APPETIZERS

This recipe is truly international. The result is a crossing between Karelian pastry (dough), meat pie (filling) and Italian cannelloni (shape). A gastronomic wonder is the bark flour, which is a reminder of hard times in Finland. It was used instead of flour for many decades when the frost or other reasons for bad harvest destroyed the crop. The final result is not as strange as one would think. The flavours are somewhat familiar and complement each other.

Rye cannelloni and a hot consommé are extremely welcome as an appetizer on a bitterly cold winter's day.

RYE CANNELONI

CONSOMMÉ

Pour the water into a saucepan and boil the rice for approximately 20 minutes. Drain the water from the rice. Chop the onion and fry it lightly in butter in a frying pan for approximately 5 minutes. Fry the steak mince. Hard-boil two eggs. Chop the eggs and mix all ingredients. Add one raw egg and the spices. Mix well. Taste for flavour.

Stir the different kinds of flours and salt into the lukewarm water. Knead the dough for a few minutes. Leave to rest for a while. Roll out the dough into a 2–3 mm (0.1 inch) thick layer and cut into about 12 x 20 cm (5 x 8 inch) pieces. Place two heaped tablespoonfuls of filling along the longer side of the piece of dough. Wet the

edges of the dough and roll the cannelloni into a cylinder shape. Brush the surface with melted butter. Bake in the oven in 250 °C (480 °F) for 10–15 minutes. Brush the surface again with a mixture of butter and milk as soon as you take the cannelloni out of the oven to prevent them from going dry.

Serve with consommé seasoned with parsley.

Tip: bark flour is not necessary for making these delicious cannelloni. If not available, use rye flour instead.

A dry sherry tastes good with the consommé, for instance **Emilio Lustao Peninsula Palo Cortado.**

FILLING:
300 ML (1 ¼ CUPS) PUDDING RICE
600 ML (20 FL OZ) WATER
500 G (18 OZ/1.1 LB) STEAK MINCE
3 EGGS
100 ML (⅖ CUP) CHOPPED PARSLEY
1 ONION
1 TEASPOON BUTTER
50 ML (1.7 FL OZ) CREAM
½ TEASPOON GROUND PAPRIKA
SALT
BLACK PEPPER CORNS

DOUGH:
200 ML (6.8 FL OZ) WATER
350 ML (1 ½ CUPS) RYE FLOUR
100 ML (⅖ CUP) PLAIN WHEAT FLOUR
50 ML (3 TABLESPOONS) BARK FLOUR
SALT

The blini is a traditional Russian delicacy. It has been known to the Finns even before the year 1809, when Finland became an autonomous part of the Russian empire. For decades, the Karelians, who are a branch of the Finnish people, frequently travelled along the Karelian isthmus to St. Petersburg and to the shores of lake Ladoga. This way the Finnish cuisine became influenced by the way of Russian cooking. After the second world war 400,000 Karelians were evacuated to the rest of Finland and settled there, and brought with them delicacies like Karelian pastries and the blini, which today are enjoyed in the whole of the country. At the beginning of last century Russian immigrants also played a major part in the promotion of the blini to Finland.

BLINI PANCAKES

500 ML (17 FL OZ) MILK
25 G (0.9 OZ) FRESH YEAST
200 ML (⅘ CUP) BUCKWHEAT FLOUR
200 ML (⅘ CUP) PLAIN WHEAT FLOUR
2 EGGS
1 TEASPOON SALT
100 ML (3.4 FL OZ) SOUR MILK
80 G (2.8 OZ) BUTTER FOR FRYING

Soak the yeast in the lukewarm milk. Add the two kinds of flour. Cover the bowl containing the batter with a towel and allow to prove for at least three hours. Add the sour milk, salt and egg yolks. Using an electric hand held mixer, whisk the egg whites until very stiff and add them to the batter. Stir the batter again lightly before frying.

Fry in plenty of butter in a blini pan to pancakes about 1 cm (0.4 inch) thick. Serve with e.g. salad of mushrooms (forest mushrooms, chopped onions and Russian-style sour cream, smetana), different kinds of roe and smetana.

*Blini pancakes are very nourishing and are eaten mostly in the autumn and the winter. Champagne will add a flavour of festivity to the cold and dark season. **Bollinger Special Cuvée** is an excellent companion to blini pancakes.*

Pelmeni and ravioli are in theory the same thing. The pelmeni are Russian and the ravioli come from Italy. Even if the Italian version nowadays is more well-known than the Russian one, the pelmeni, due to the proximity of Russia, have a fixed place especially in the cuisine of eastern Finland.

Although the pelmeni, due to their many stages of preparation, are quite time-consuming to make, the delicious flavour is worth the trouble. The mildly aniseed-flavoured fennel complements the rich world of flavours of this recipe.

CRAYFISH PELMENI

CLEAR FENNEL BROTH

DOUGH:
100 ML (3.4 FL OZ) WATER
1 EGG
400 ML (1 5/8 CUPS) PLAIN WHITE FLOUR
A PINCH OF SALT

FILLING:
250 G (9 OZ) TAILS OF CRAYFISH
DILL
50 ML (1.7 FL OZ) RUSSIAN-STYLE SOUR
CREAM, SMETANA
½ ONION

BROTH:
1 LITRE (2.1 PT) WATER
½ VEGETABLE STOCK CUBE
1 FENNEL
1 CARROT
1 ONION
1 TABLESPOON OIL
1 BAY LEAF
3 DRIED ALLSPICE BERRIES
SALT

Mix the ingredients of the dough and knead for about five minutes in order to make the dough elastic. Allow to rest for 30 minutes.

Chop the onion finely. Fry lightly in oil in a frying pan. Set aside to cool. Chop the crayfish tails with a knife or in a food processor.

Mix the onion, crayfish meat, chopped dill and smetana into an even paste.

Boil the water and add half a vegetable stock cube. Chop the vegetables roughly and add them to the stock along with the spices. Leave to simmer on low heat for approximately 45–60 minutes. Strain the stock until it is clear and add a pinch of salt, if necessary. Taste for flavour.

Roll out the dough on a board until it is approximately 2 mm (0.1 inch) thick. Cut into rounds with a crinkled cutter. Place a teaspoonful of filling on each piece of dough. Wet the edges of the dough and make a half-moon shaped pocket. If you wish, you can also fold the straight corners of the half-moon to make the pelmeni a bundle resembling a tortellini. Cook the pelmeni in a litre of boiling water for about 10 minutes. Lift the ready pelmeni into the fennel broth, decorate with dill and serve.

Nikolai Wheat Lager *would be a good choice with the Unmalted wheat that has been used in this beer gives additional freshness to its flavor and makes it an excellent companion with Crayfish Pelmenis.*

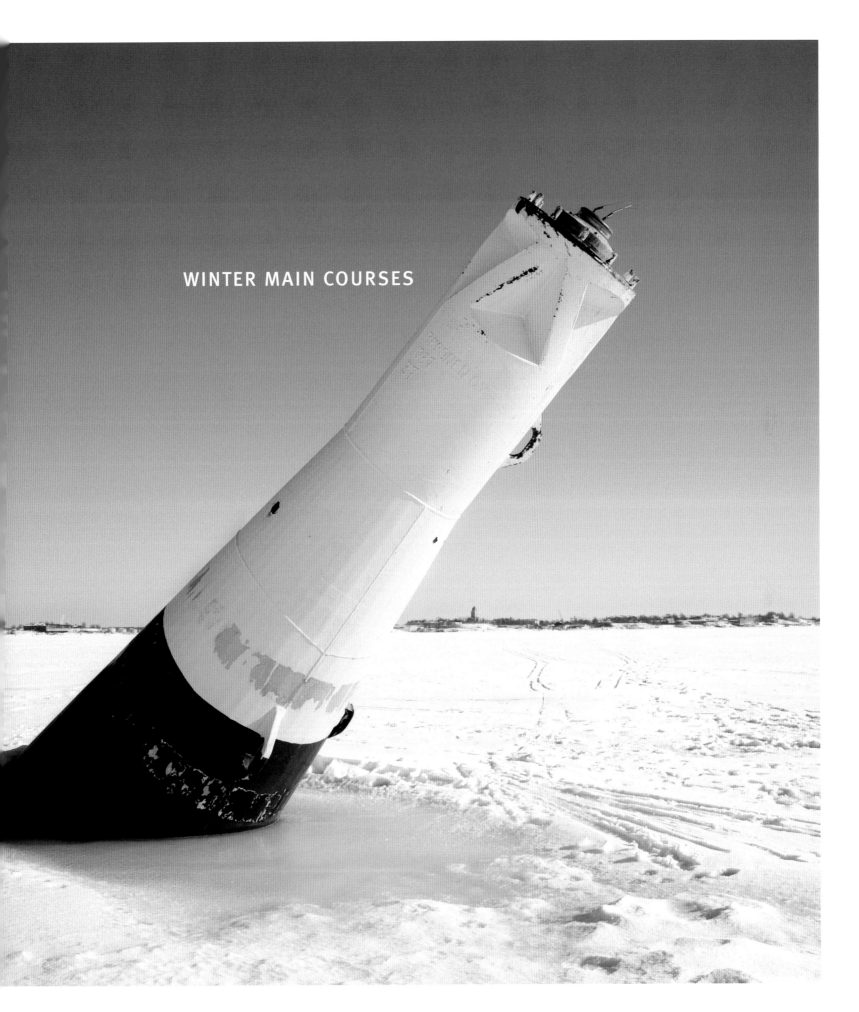

WINTER MAIN COURSES

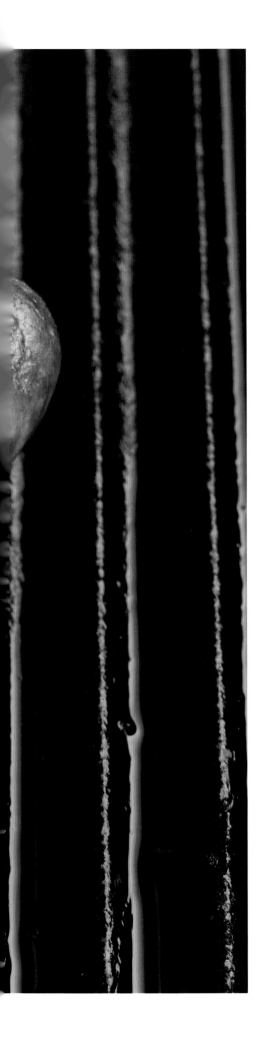

Making sausages requires the right equipment and quite some energy. Buying a mincer pays off, as home-made sausages are twice as good as ready-made ones.

The rabbit sausages spiced with herbs are a bit like the German Thüringer Bratwurst. The difference lies in the game-like taste of the rabbit, which makes the sausages of this recipe a rare delicacy.

In Finland sausages are traditionally served with potato salad. As this is no ordinary pork sausage, the potato salad has been substituted by a slightly more special dish: fried Jerusalem artichokes.

RABBIT SAUSAGES

FRIED JERUSALEM ARTICHOKES

SAUSAGES:
500 G (18 OZ/1.1 LB) RABBIT MEAT
500 G (18 OZ/1.1 LB) LOIN OR SIDE OF
PORK
INTESTINES
1 ONION
1 TEASPOON GROUND PEPPER
FRESH MAJORAM
FRESH ROSEMARY
FRESH THYME
½ TEASPOON GROUND WHITE PEPPER
½ TEASPOON GROUND NUTMEG
1 BAY LEAF
SALT

FRIED JERUSALEM ARTICHOKES:
400 G (14 OZ) JERUSALEM ARTICHOKES
1 TABLESPOON LEMON JUICE
30 G (1 OZ) BUTTER
SALT

Cut the meat from the bones and remove the membranes. Rinse and mince the meat in a mincer together with the pork. You can mince the onion at the same time. In this way the rabbit meat will not stick as the onion will help it through the mincer. Mix the meats and add the spices. Mince the mixture another two times.

Put the intestines in cold water about half an hour before use. Put the sausage meat through the mincer again and via a sausage funnel into the intestine. Make the sausages approximately 15–20 cm (8 inch) long.

Prick small holes into the sausages using e.g. a needle. Simmer in water seasoned with salt and a bay leaf for approximately 10 minutes. Set aside and cook in a grill pan or under the grill of the cooker.

Peel and chop the Jerusalem artichokes into pieces the size of the tip of your thumb. Squeeze lemon juice over them so they will not darken. Fry in butter in a frying pan and season with salt.

Serve with the rabbit sausages.

*A good companion to rabbit sausages is **Karhu III**. This lager has body enough to accompany the rich tastes of Rabbit sausages and slightly sweet Jerusalem artichokes.*

This fish pie under a rye cover, "patakukko" or "kalakukko" as it is also called, is a typical dish from eastern Finland, from the Savo-district. The recipe is well-known also outside Savo and is nowadays enjoyed in the whole country. "Patakukko" can be eaten hot as well as cold.

PATAKUKKO

Mix the cool water, the flour and salt. Knead for a while and add the melted butter. Set aside.

Gut and wash the vendace. Cover the bottom of a casserole dish with some of the vendace. Sprinkle a bit of salt on them. Put a layer of pork or bacon on top of the vendace and add another layer of vendace. Repeat until the casserole is almost full. Shape the dough into a cover for the casserole dish. Make it a little bit less than 1 cm (0.4 inch) thick. Prick the dough with a fork and brush it with melted butter.

Cook in the oven at 200 °C (390 °F) until the cover becomes brownish. After this, turn down the heat to 150 °C (300 °F). If there is a risk for the rye cover to become too dry, cover the patakukko with foil. The patakukko is ready after cooking in the oven for 2 hours, but the flavour is better the longer you keep the patakukko in the oven at low temperature. In order for the dough not to get hard when you take the patakukko from the oven, brush it with a mix of melted butter and milk and cover with a towel for at least 15 minutes.

Tip: If you want a stronger rye flavour to your patakukko, line the casserole with rye dough before filling it with the vendace and the pork meat.

*A suitable drink to this traditional meal is **butter milk.***

FILLING:
1½ KG (3.3 LB) VENDACE
300 G (11 OZ) SLICED SIDE OF PORK OR SLICED SMOKED STREAKY BACON
SALT

DOUGH:
400 ML (13.5 FL OZ) WATER
700 ML (2 7/8 CUPS) RYE FLOUR
250 ML (1 CUP) PLAIN WHEAT FLOUR
80 G (2.8 OZ) MELTED BUTTER
A PINCH OF SALT

The story of Karelian stew is to a large degree equal to that of another well-known traditional Karelian dish, the Karelian pastry. The word "Karelian" has been added to the names of the dishes only when they have been served in other parts of Finland as well. Karelian stew and Karelian pastries have another thing in common, too. They started conquering the culinary world only after the second world war.

KARELIAN STEW

ROOT VEGETABLES IN BEER

400 G (14 OZ) BEEF, E.G. SIRLOIN
400 G (14 OZ) LOIN OR OUTER FILLET OF PORK
10 DRIED ALLSPICE BERRIES
3 BAY LEAVES
1 TEASPOON SALT
WATER

ROOT VEGETABLES IN BEER:
150 G (5.3 OZ) POTATOES
150 G (5.3 OZ) SWEDE
100 G (3.5 OZ) TURNIP
1 ONION
2 CARROTS
100 ML (3.4 FL OZ) TREACLE
100 ML (3.4 FL OZ) BEER
SALT

Rinse the meat and remove the membranes. Cut the beef into fairly bit chunks. Put the chunks and the spices into a cast iron casserole dish. Add enough water to almost cover the meat. Put the dish in the oven at 225 °C (440 °F). Do not cover. When the upper chunks of meat start getting brown, turn down the heat to 160 °C (320 °F). Leave the meat in the oven for approximately three more hours and stir from time to time so the upper chunks of meat do not become dry.

Wash and peel the vegetables. Chop them into pieces the size of your fingertip. Place the vegetables in an ovenproof dish and pour the treacle and the beer on them. Add salt. Cook in the oven at 170 °C (340 °F) for about 1 ½ hour stirring the vegetables from time to time.

Tip: As an alternative to the root vegetables, you can also serve boiled potatoes.

Le Baronnie Madeleine, *a red wine from the Chinon district in the Loire valley in France, will go well with this traditional Finnish dish.*

WINTER DESSERTS

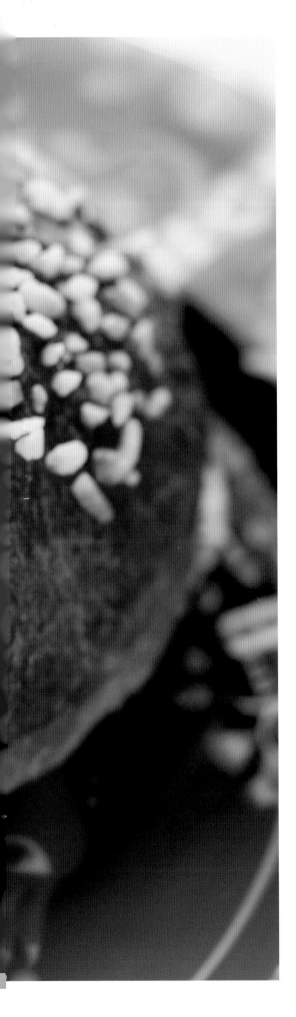

Shrovetide and lent is a celebration during the coldest part of winter. In central Europe and in many other catholic countries a colourful carnival is part of lent. In Finland and in the other Scandinavian countries lent is celebrated outdoors, especially sledging or skiing down snowy slopes. Part of the Scandinavian culinary lent tradition are the buns described above, enjoyed with a hot drink, and for main course, pea soup is often enjoyed. The modern and slightly more up-market version you will find on page 43 of this book.

SHROVE BUN "PULLA"

COCOA-FLAVOURED COFFEE

Crumble the yeast into the tepid milk. Add the beaten eggs, the sugar, the salt and the cardamom. Pour part of the flour into the mix and stir well until it forms a thick gloop. Beat the mixture well for a minute or two and add the rest of the flour little by little stirring occasionally. Add the cool melted butter/margarine and stir the mixture well for a while. If it is still too thin, add some more flour. Knead the dough for approximately 5 minutes. Leave the dough to rest and allow it to rise in a large dish for approximately 30 minutes. Cover the dish with a towel.

Turn the dough onto a floured board, and shape the dough into fist-sized balls, rolling them between the palm of your hand and the board. Place them on a baking tray. Brush each one with some beaten egg and sprinkle sugar nibs on top. Bake in the oven at 220 °C (430 °F) for 10–15 minutes or until the buns are beautifully brown.

Hull the raspberries and blueberries and rinse them well. Put the berries into a saucepan and add 50 ml (1.7 fl oz) water. Pour the sugar into the saucepan just before the mix starts boiling, stirring well. Boil the jam for 10–15 minutes stirring occasionally. Skim the froth off the jam and leave to cool for an

PULLA:
500 ML (17 FL OZ) MILK
50 G (1.8 OZ) FRESH YEAST
300 ML (1 ¼ CUPS) SUGAR
2 EGGS
1 TEASPOON GROUND CARDAMOM
½ TEASPOON SALT
1200–1300 ML (5–5 ⅔ CUPS) PLAIN WHEAT FLOUR
150 G (5.3 OZ) MARGARINE OR BUTTER

RASPBERRY-BLUEBERRY JAM:
250 G (9 OZ) RASPBERRIES
250 G (9 OZ) BLUEBERRIES
250 G (9 OZ) PRESERVING SUGAR

200 ML (6.8 FL OZ) DOUBLE CREAM
1 TEASPOON SUGAR
500 ML (17 FL OZ) COFFEE
500 ML (17 FL OZ) COCOA

hour. Pour the jam into clean jars or use it straight away for filling the halved buns.

Whip the chilled double cream until it forms firm peaks and add the sugar. Cut the buns into halves lengthwise and dig a small hole into the middle of the lower halves. Put a heaped teaspoon of raspberry-blueberry jam into the holes and pipe a ring of whipped cream round the jam.

Mix the hot coffee with the hot cocoa. Add milk and sugar, if required.

Tokay is a Hungarian sweet dessert wine. Its refined taste comes from blue mould which emerges on the surface of over-ripe grapes during the first frosty nights of the autumn.

Thus the great wine of Hungarians, related to the Finnish people, will be an excellent companion to the mixed fruit soup. Rice porridge and mixed fruit soup are Christmas-time dishes. They are found in many Finnish homes especially on Christmas Eve on the breakfast or lunch tables. This light Christmas luncheon, differing from the traditional every-day lunch, allows you to be ready for the strong and versatile supper on Christmas Eve.

TOKAY-MIXED FRUIT SOUP

RICE PORRIDGE

TOKAY-MIXED FRUIT SOUP:
1½ LITRE (3.2 PT) WATER
300 ML (10 FL OZ) TOKAY DESSERT WINE
120 G (4.2 OZ) DRIED APRICOTS
120 G (4.2 OZ) PRUNES
50 G (1.8 OZ) RAISINS
150 ML (⅗ CUP) SUGAR
3 CINNAMON STICKS
4 TABLESPOONS POTATO FLOUR

RICE PORRIDGE:
250 ML (1 CUP) PUDDING RICE
250 ML (8.5 FL OZ) WATER
1 LITRE (2.1 PT) MILK
1 TEASPOON SALT

Pour half of the water and Tokay into a saucepan. Add the fruit. Leave to soak for a couple of hours. Put the saucepan on the cooker and add the sugar and cinnamon sticks. Simmer for approximately 45 minutes. Thicken the soup with a mixture of potato flour, the rest of the Tokay and water. Pour the mixture slowly into the saucepan stirring all the time. Bring to the boil. Serve with rice porridge.

Pour the rice into boiling water. Cook until the water has been absorbed. Add the milk. Simmer for approximately an hour. Stir frequently, at least to begin with, so the porridge will not burn and stick to the saucepan. Add salt and taste for flavour.

*The Hungarian dessert wine Tokay is a natural choice as a wine recommended to complement this dish. **Tokaji Aszú Eszencia** is refined with a taste of apricots and raisins.*

Cheesecakes are slightly time-consuming and require patience to make, but the final result is worth the trouble. In this recipe the blueberries give the cheesecake not only its flavour, but also its colour. Filtering the berries through a linen cloth or a coffee filter produces a juice which is beautifully uniform in colour and totally free of lumps.

BLUEBERRY CHEESE-CAKE

BASE:
200 G (7 OZ) DIGESTIVE BISCUITS
80 G (2.8 OZ) BUTTER

FILLING:
1 LITRE (8.4 CUPS) BLUEBERRIES
100 ML (3.4 FL OZ) WATER
5 SHEETS OF GELATIN
600 G (21 OZ/1.3 LB) CREAM CHEESE
400 ML (13.5 FL OZ) DOUBLE CREAM
200 ML (6.8 FL OZ) (⅘ CUP) SUGAR
1½ TABLESPOONS VANILLA SUGAR
1 TABLESPOON LEMON JUICE
ICING SUGAR

Crush the biscuits into crumbs using a food processor. Mix with the melted butter into an even paste. Press the paste into the bottom of a dish with a detachable base covered with baking paper. The biscuit base should be approximately 5 mm (0.2 inch) thick.

Pour the water and blueberries into a saucepan. Pulp the berries with e.g. a pestle. Boil for a while. Strain through a coffee filter, this gives you a clear blueberry juice. Pour the juice back into the saucepan. Soak the gelatin sheets in cold water for about five minutes. Squeeze the water out of them and add them to the blueberry juice at a low temperature. Wait until the gelatin melts. Allow to cool.

Whip the cream. Mix the cream, cheese, sugar, lemon juice, blueberry juice and whipped cream. Stir until the mixture becomes evenly purple. Cover the biscuit base with the mixture. Smooth over the surface of the mixture with a spatula. Allow to rest in its dish in the fridge for at least four hours or overnight. Decorate with blueberries and icing sugar.

Grahams 10 yrs. Tawny port is an exquisite companion to blueberries.

EPILOGUE

The creators of this book are two friends: Kimmo Saira and myself, Tero Kallio. The photographs and layout are created by Kimmo. The recipes are a result of my choices and ideas, as well as the cooking and the text of the book.

Our first book presenting Austrian and Scandinavian dishes got an excellent reception which spurred us onto a new project. The first meetings and brainstorms concerning this book were held as early as in the autumn of 2005. It was clear to both Kimmo and myself that we would aim higher this time. We wanted to make this new book more comprehensive as well as more enjoyable regarding its visual appearance.

The theme was also clear from the very beginning. As the theme of our first book was about Scandinavian and Finnish food culture, now we wanted to open the window to the Finnish charac-ter as a whole. When investigating the market of cookery books we found to our surprise that litera-ture regarding Finnish or Scandinavian cooking, past or present, either in Finnish or in English, was extremely limited. A few recipes are mentioned in some books, but Finnish and Scandinavian cuisines as a compiled and independent theme seem to have been sadly neglected.

Apart from the Finnish theme it was our goal

to make our new book an original and personal one. This is why we did not limit ourselves to presenting only "ancient" traditional Finnish dishes or more modern ones known from other contexts. They have their place in this book, too, but by developing well-known traditional dishes and inventing totally new ones we wanted to leave our footprint on the culinary map of the world.

The planning of this book, the cooking of the meals, the photography, the suggestions for drinks, the translation as well as the printing and marketing of the book have taken many days of hard work. The book was created during weekends and summer holidays, as both Kimmo and myself are employed elsewhere. In addition to our own contribution Gunilla Markkola, Johanna McDonald and Andrei Donoghue have given us much appreciated help in translating the book from Finnish into English, and Henry Johansson assisted us with the drink selection.

We also extend our warm thanks to our colleagues Tmi Gastrologi, Iittala Ltd and Main-Domain Ltd, for their help and cooperation.

Helsinki 1st July 2008
Tero Kallio

INDEX

INFORMATION

www.raikaskustannus.fi
myynti@raikaskustannus.fi